GRAPHIC LIBRARY™

GRAPHIC SCIENCE

# ADVENTURES IN SOUND

WITH MAX AXIOM™ SUPER SCIENTIST

An Augmented Reading Science Experience

by Emily Sohn | illustrated by Cynthia Martin and Anne Timmons

Consultant:
Dr. Ronald Browne
Associate Professor of Elementary Education
Minnesota State University, Mankato

CAPSTONE PRESS
a capstone imprint

Graphic Library is published by Capstone Press,
1710 Roe Crest Drive, North Mankato, Minnesota 56003.
www.mycapstone.com

Copyright © 2019 by Capstone Press.
All rights reserved. No part of this publication may be reproduced in whole or in part, or stored in a retrieval system, or transmitted in any form or by any means, electronic, mechanical, photocopying, recording, or otherwise, without written permission of the publisher.

Library of Congress Cataloging-in-Publication Data is available on the Library of Congress website.

ISBN: 978-1-5435-2944-9 (library binding)
ISBN: 978-1-5435-2955-5 (paperback)
ISBN: 978-1-5435-2965-4 (eBook PDF)

Summary: In graphic novel format, follows the adventures of Max Axiom as he explains the science behind sound.

*Art Director and Designer*
Bob Lentz

*Colorist*
Michael Kelleher

*Cover Artist*
Tod Smith

*Editor*
Christopher L. Harbo

Photo Credits
Capstone/Scott Thoms: 8; Capstone Studio/Karon Dubke: 29

## Download the Capstone  app!

- Ask an adult to download the Capstone 4D app.
- Scan the cover and stars inside the book for additional content.

When you scan a spread, you'll find fun extra stuff to go with this book! You can also find these things on the web at www.capstone4D.com using the password: sound.29449

Printed in the United States of America.
PA017

# TABLE OF CONTENTS

**SECTION 1**
WHAT'S THAT SOUND? .............. 4

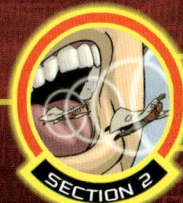
**SECTION 2**
MAKING SENSE OF THE WAVES ... 12

**SECTION 3**
WHAT SOUND CAN DO .............. 18

**SECTION 4**
LISTEN SAFELY ......................... 24

More About Sound ................................................................ 28
Shoebox Guitar ..................................................................... 29
Discussion Questions, Writing Prompts, Take a Quiz! ......... 30
Glossary ................................................................................ 31
Read More, Internet Sites, Index .......................................... 32

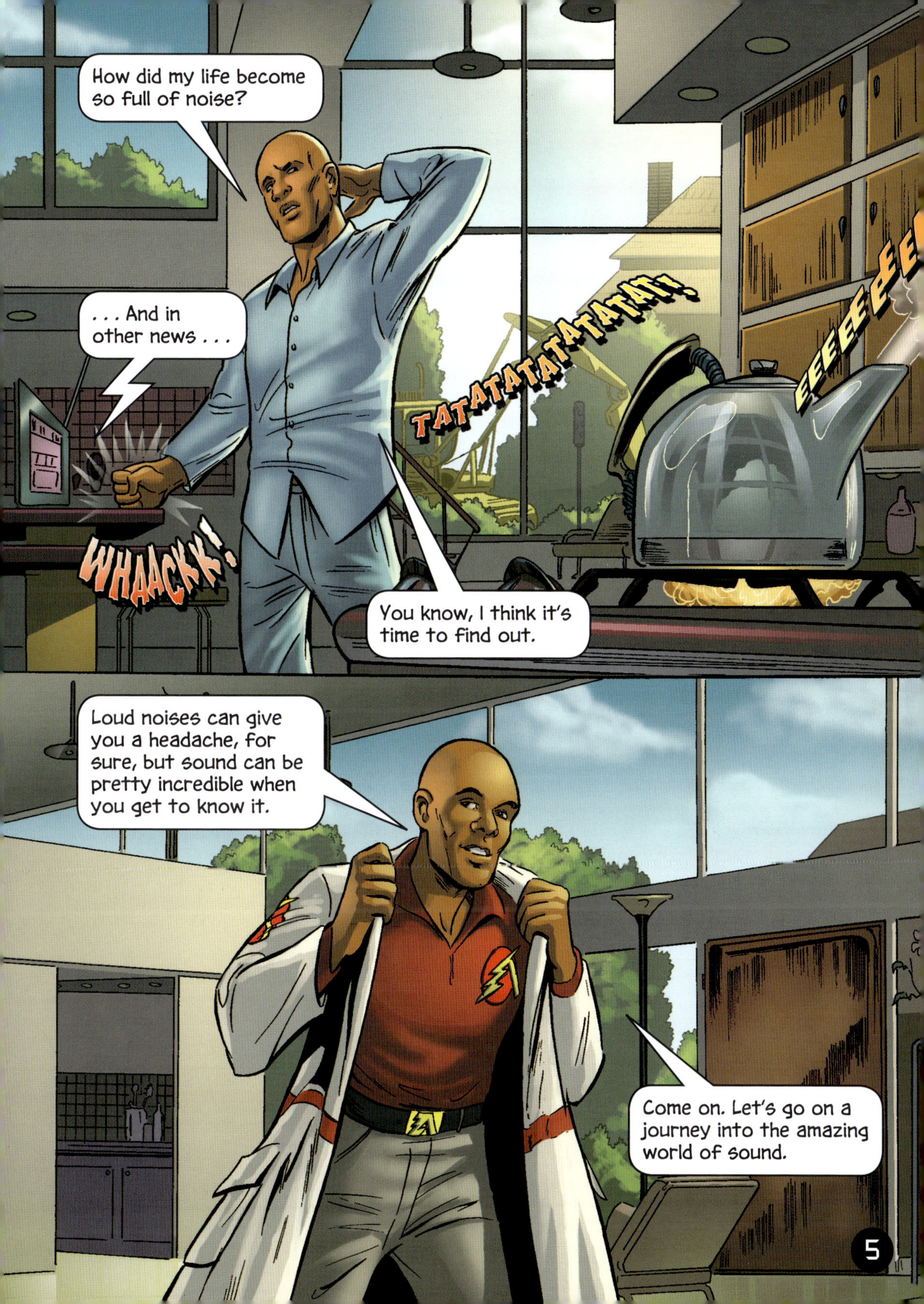
How did my life become so full of noise?
. . . And in other news . . .
WHAACKK!
TATATATATATATATAT!
EEEEEEEE
You know, I think it's time to find out.
Loud noises can give you a headache, for sure, but sound can be pretty incredible when you get to know it.
Come on. Let's go on a journey into the amazing world of sound.

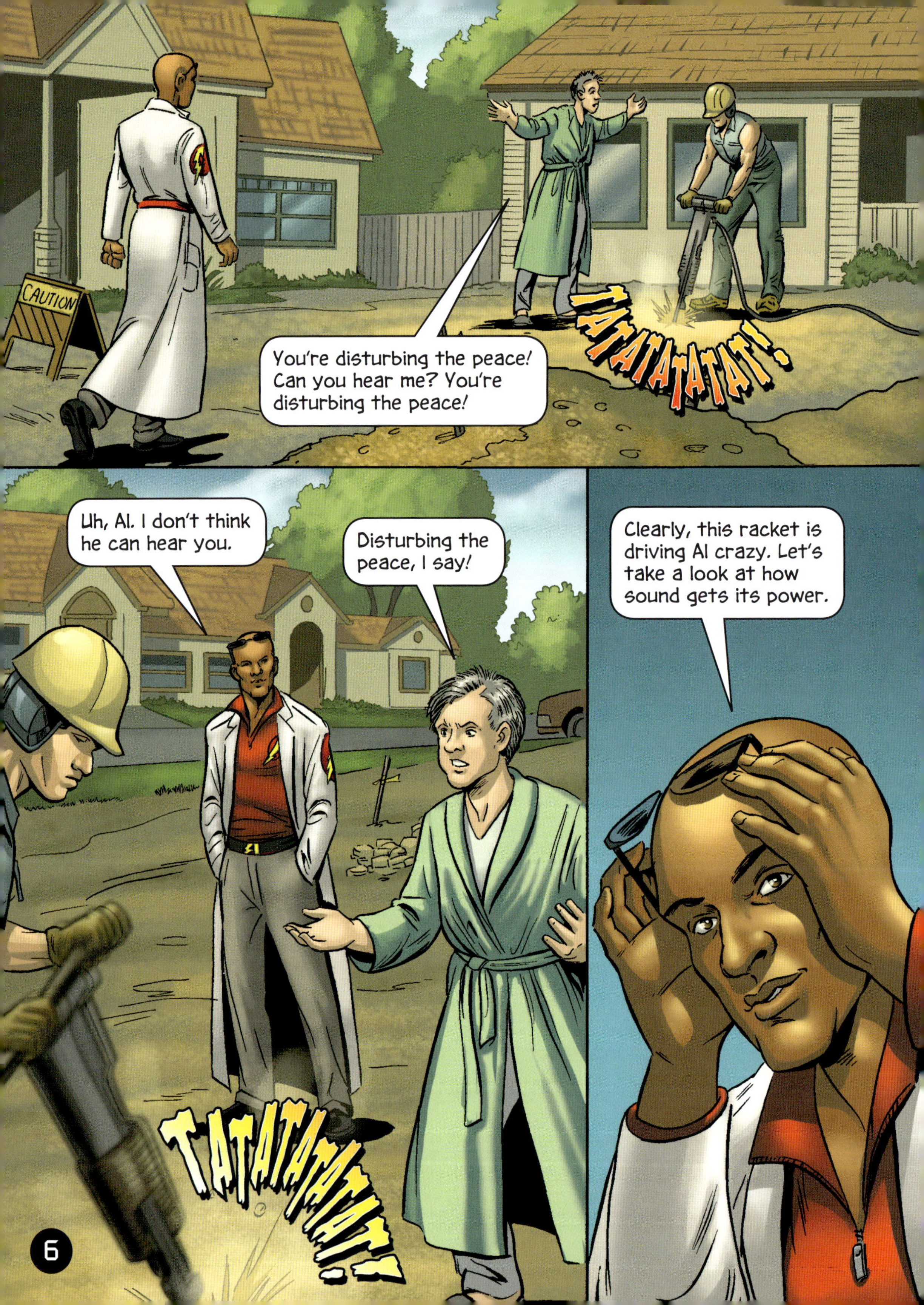
CAUTION
TATATATATAT!
You're disturbing the peace! Can you hear me? You're disturbing the peace!
Uh, Al. I don't think he can hear you.
Disturbing the peace, I say!
TATATATATAT!
Clearly, this racket is driving Al crazy. Let's take a look at how sound gets its power.

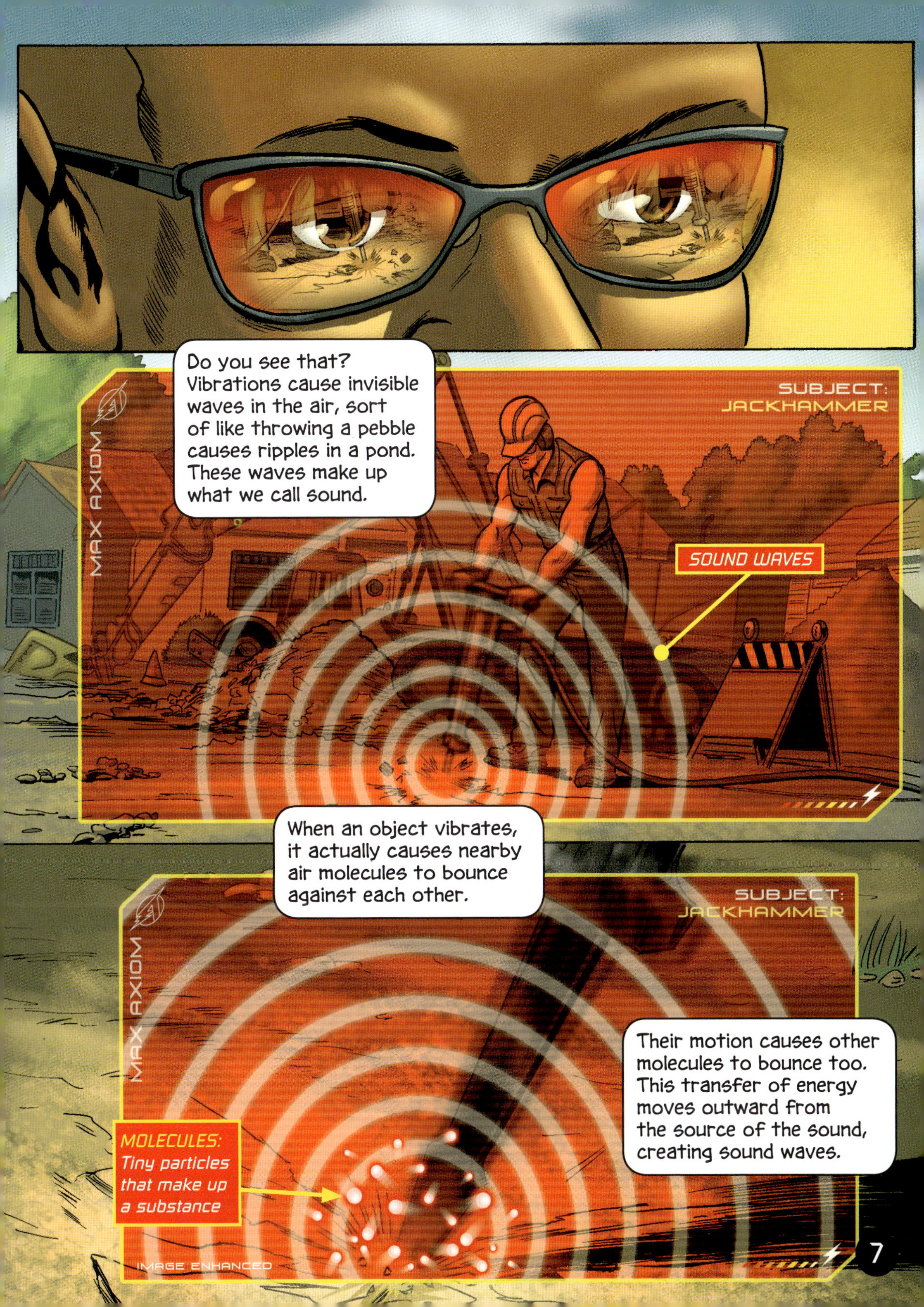
Do you see that? Vibrations cause invisible waves in the air, sort of like throwing a pebble causes ripples in a pond. These waves make up what we call sound.
MAX AXIOM
SUBJECT: JACKHAMMER
SOUND WAVES
When an object vibrates, it actually causes nearby air molecules to bounce against each other.
MAX AXIOM
SUBJECT: JACKHAMMER
Their motion causes other molecules to bounce too. This transfer of energy moves outward from the source of the sound, creating sound waves.
MOLECULES: Tiny particles that make up a substance
IMAGE ENHANCED

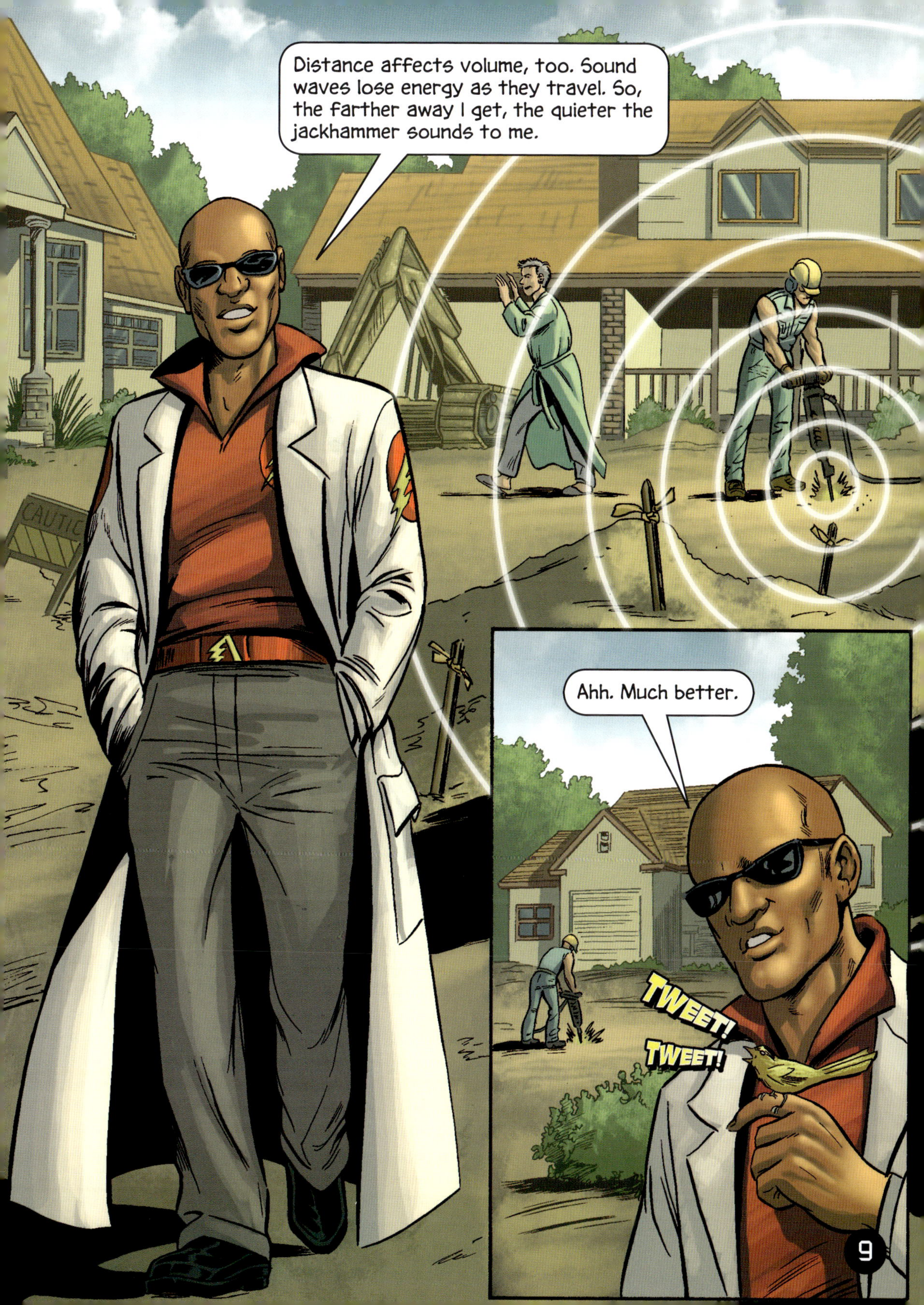
Distance affects volume, too. Sound waves lose energy as they travel. So, the farther away I get, the quieter the jackhammer sounds to me.
CAUTI
Ahh. Much better.
TWEET!
TWEET!

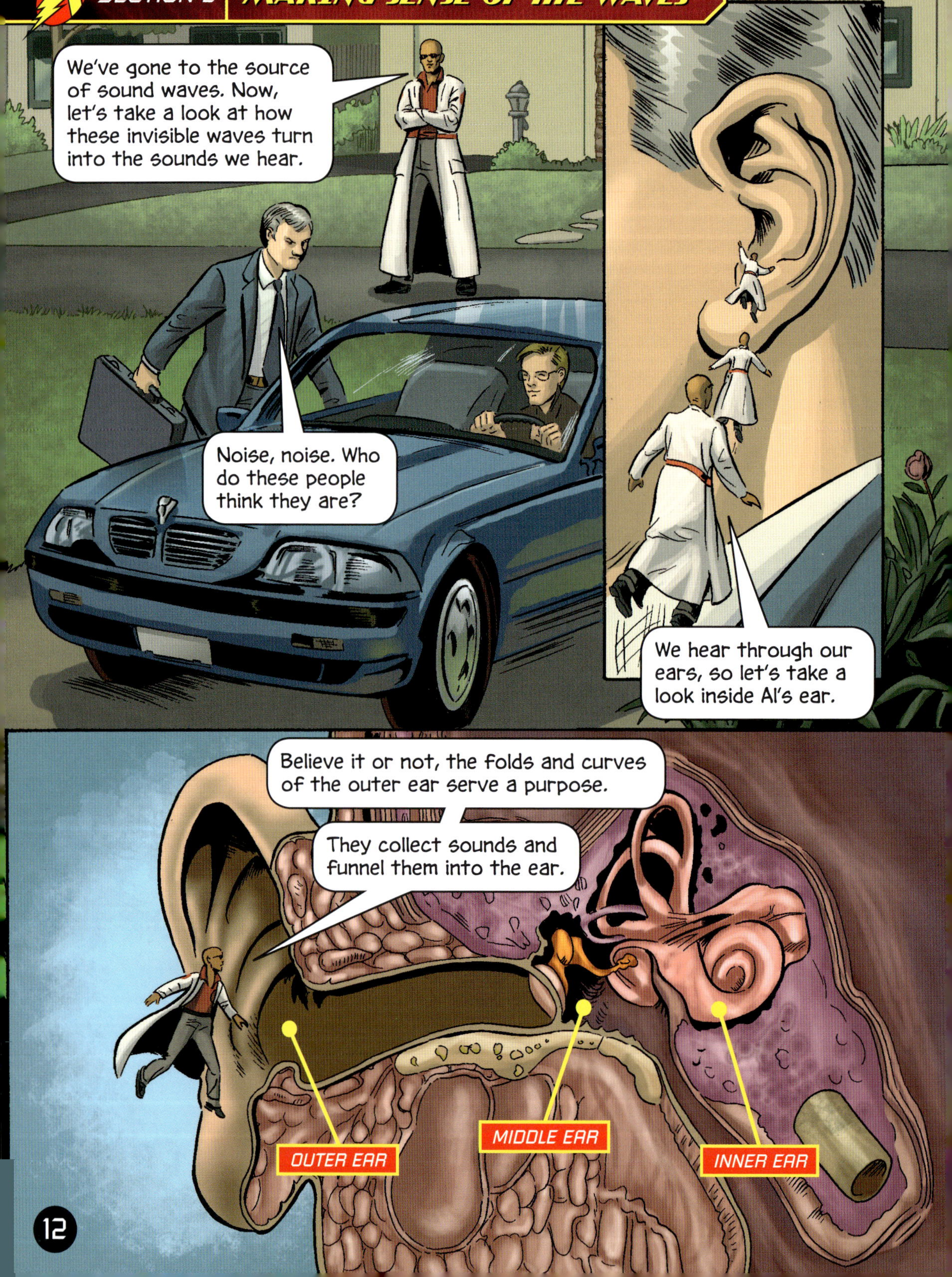
We've gone to the source of sound waves. Now, let's take a look at how these invisible waves turn into the sounds we hear.
Noise, noise. Who do these people think they are?
We hear through our ears, so let's take a look inside Al's ear.
Believe it or not, the folds and curves of the outer ear serve a purpose.
They collect sounds and funnel them into the ear.
OUTER EAR
MIDDLE EAR
INNER EAR

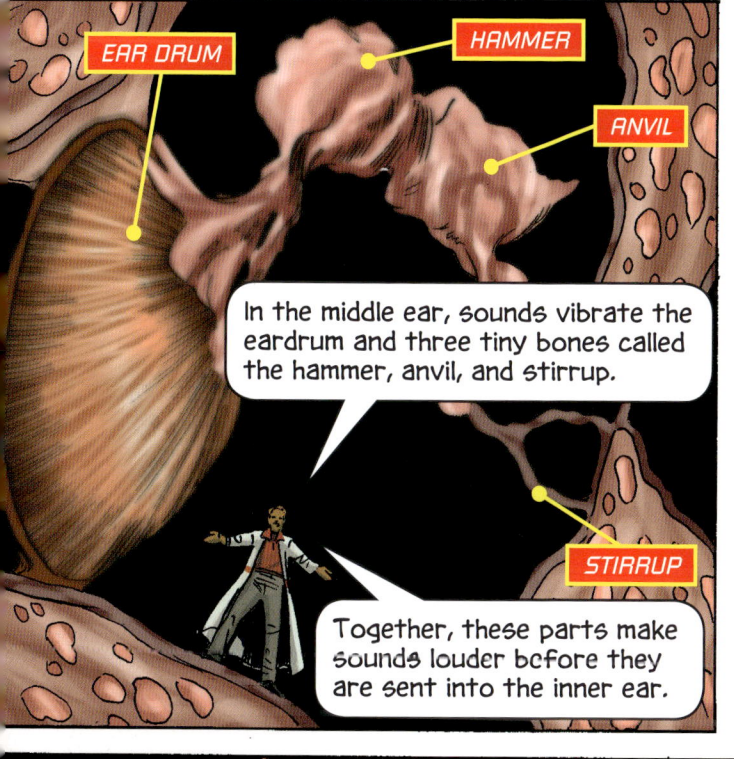
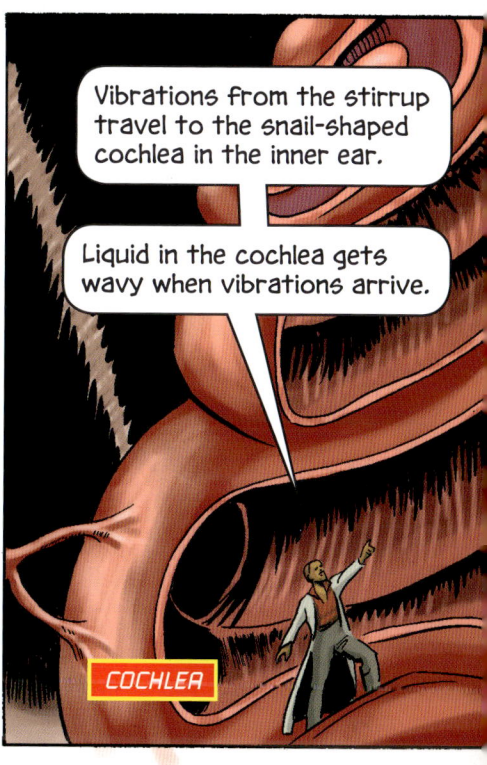

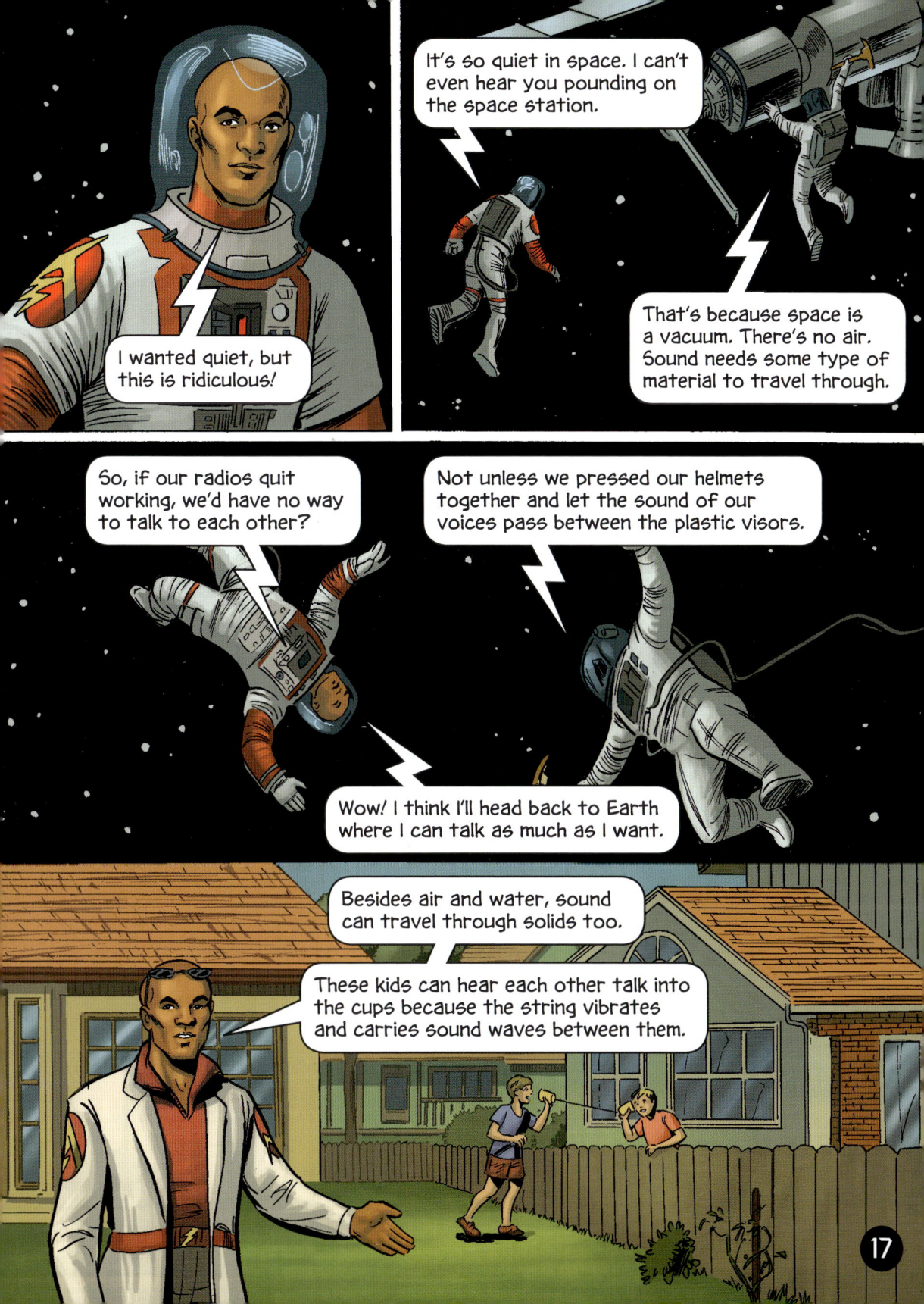

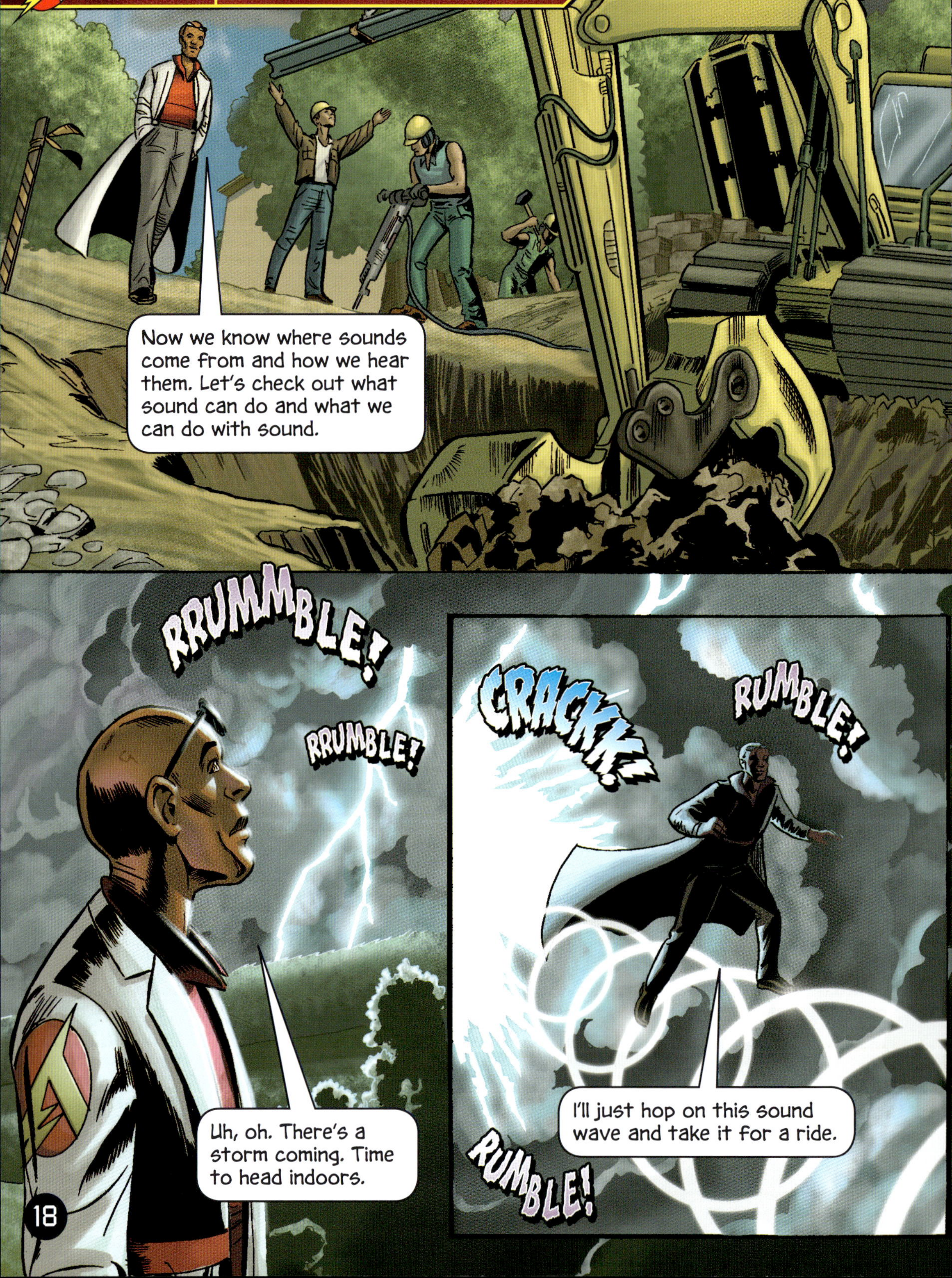
Now we know where sounds come from and how we hear them. Let's check out what sound can do and what we can do with sound.
RRUMMBLE!
RRUMBLE!
Uh, oh. There's a storm coming. Time to head indoors.
CRACKK!
RUMBLE!
I'll just hop on this sound wave and take it for a ride.
RUMBLE!

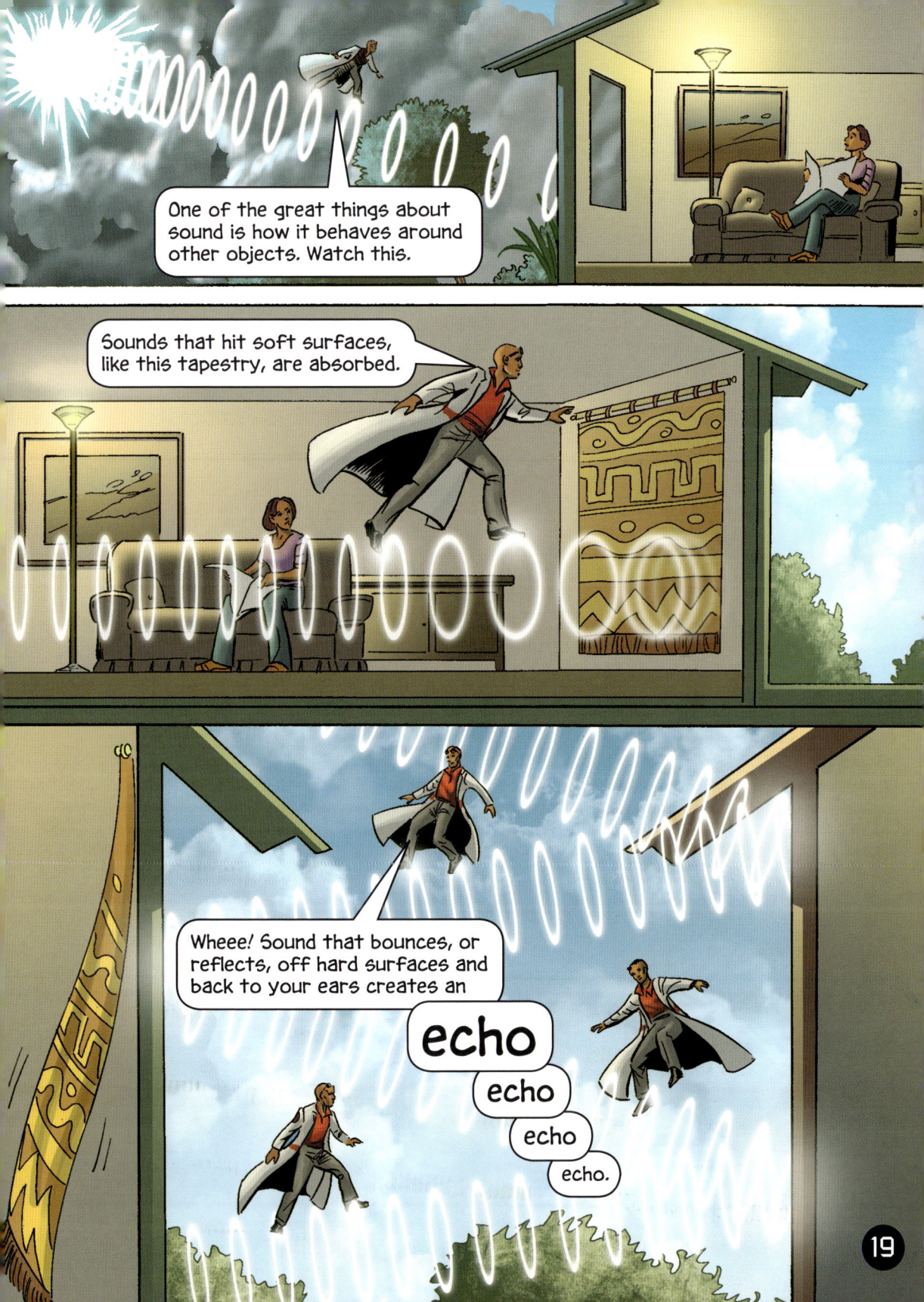

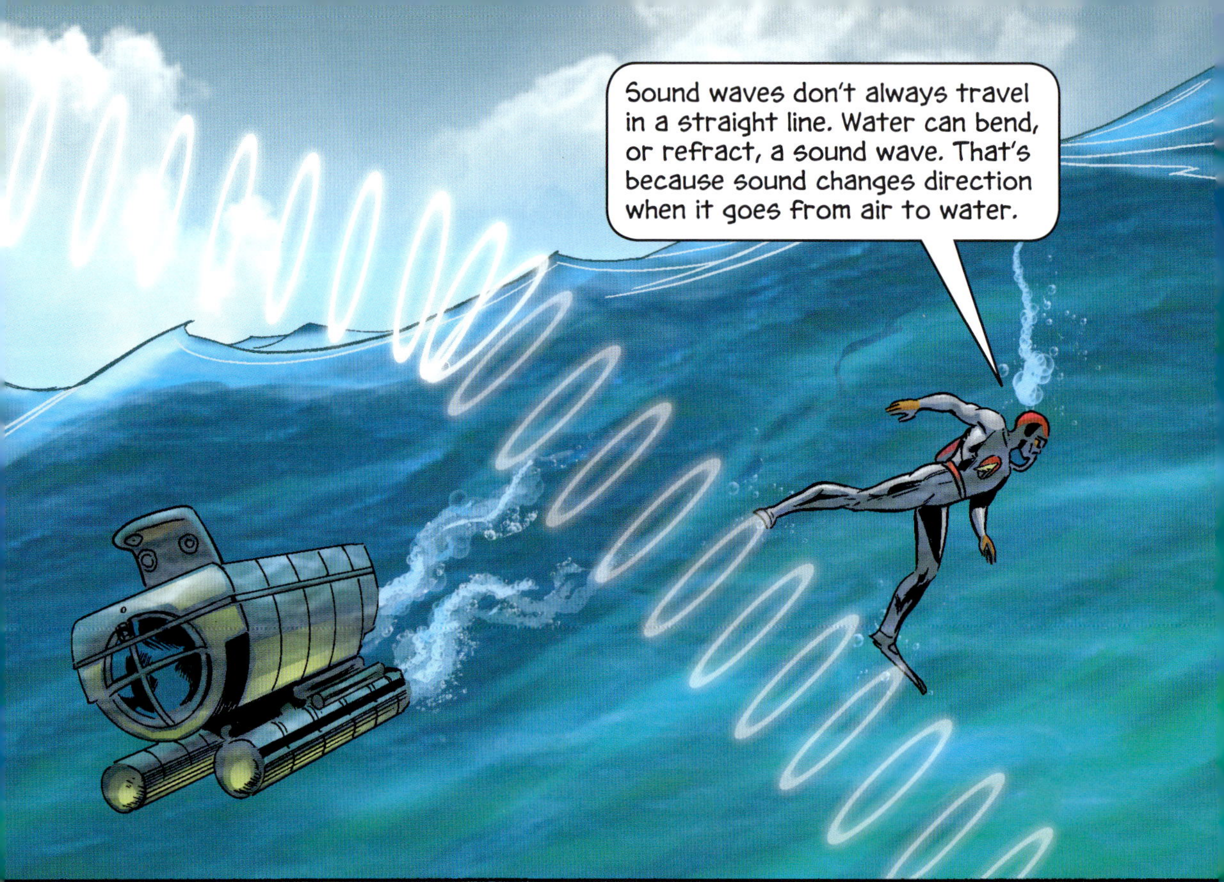
Sound waves don't always travel in a straight line. Water can bend, or refract, a sound wave. That's because sound changes direction when it goes from air to water.

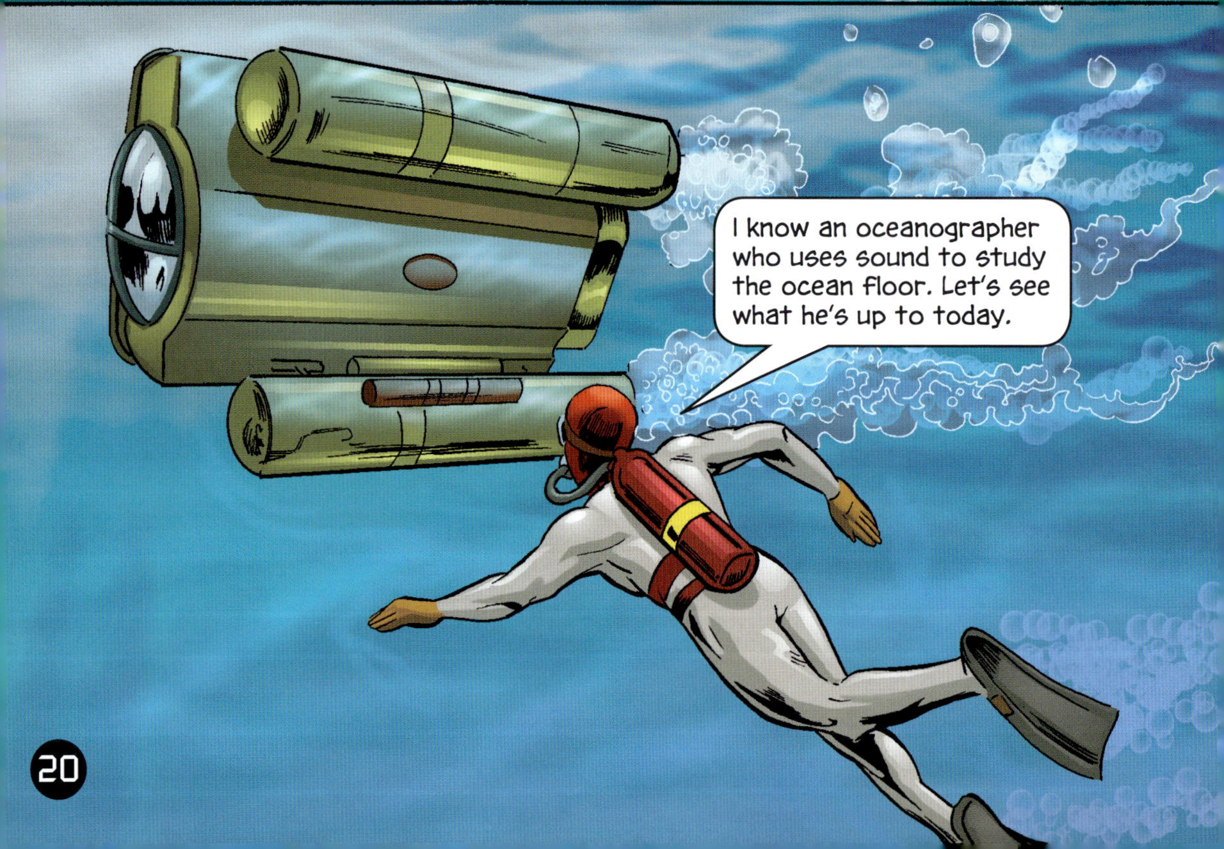
I know an oceanographer who uses sound to study the ocean floor. Let's see what he's up to today.

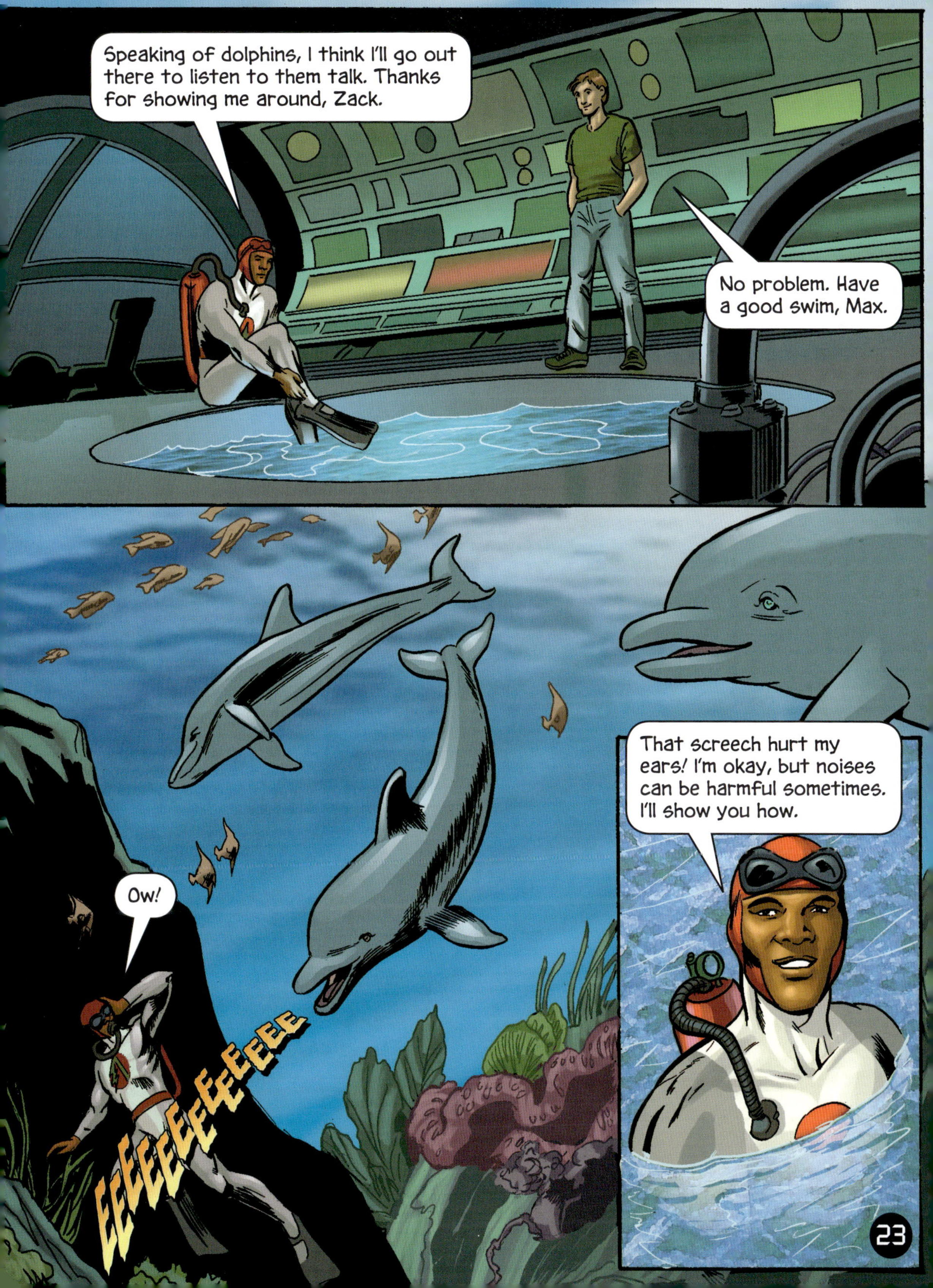
Speaking of dolphins, I think I'll go out there to listen to them talk. Thanks for showing me around, Zack.
No problem. Have a good swim, Max.
Ow!
EEEEEEEEEEEEEE
That screech hurt my ears! I'm okay, but noises can be harmful sometimes. I'll show you how.

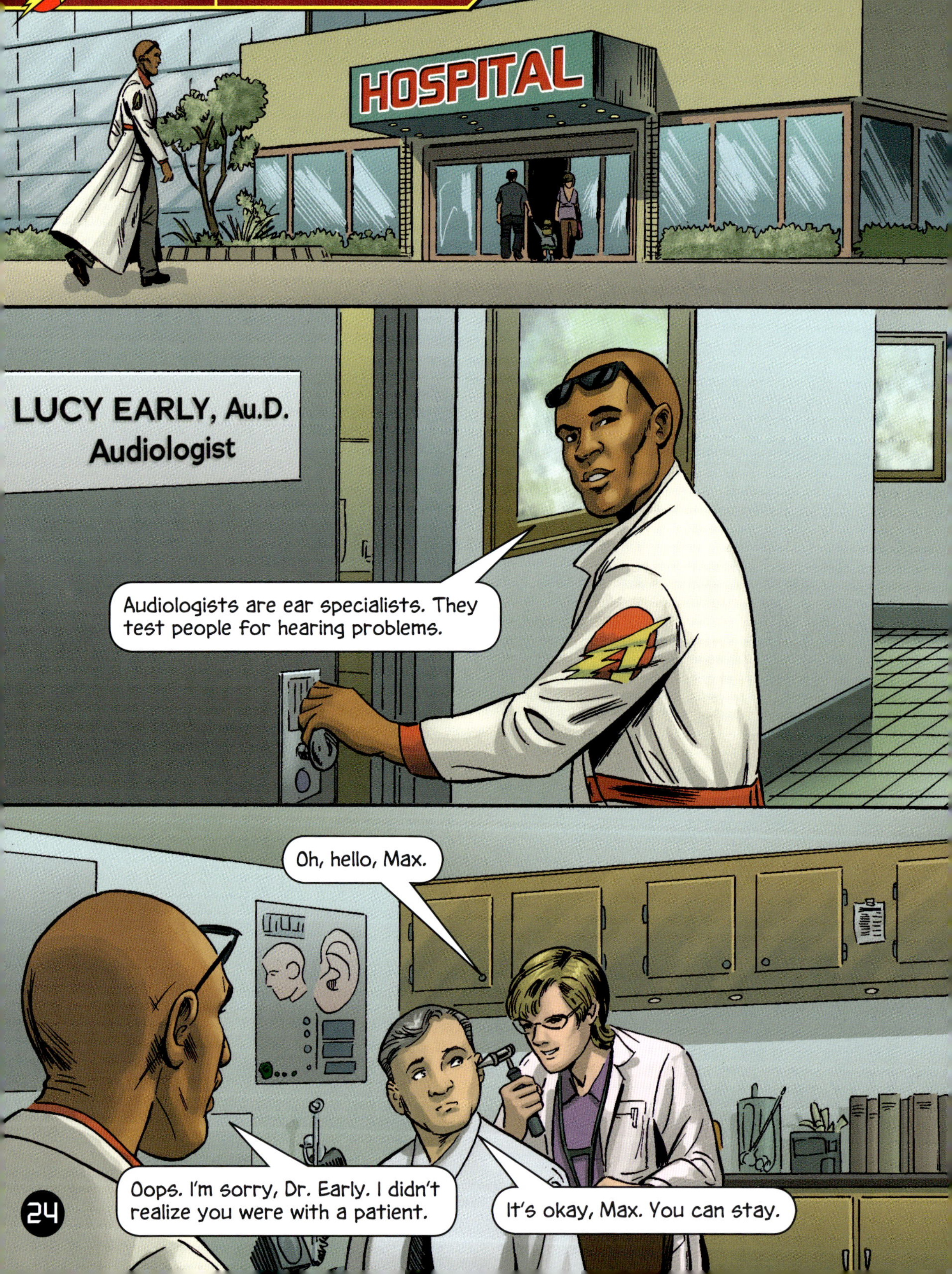
HOSPITAL
LUCY EARLY, Au.D.
Audiologist
Audiologists are ear specialists. They test people for hearing problems.
Oh, hello, Max.
Oops. I'm sorry, Dr. Early. I didn't realize you were with a patient.
It's okay, Max. You can stay.

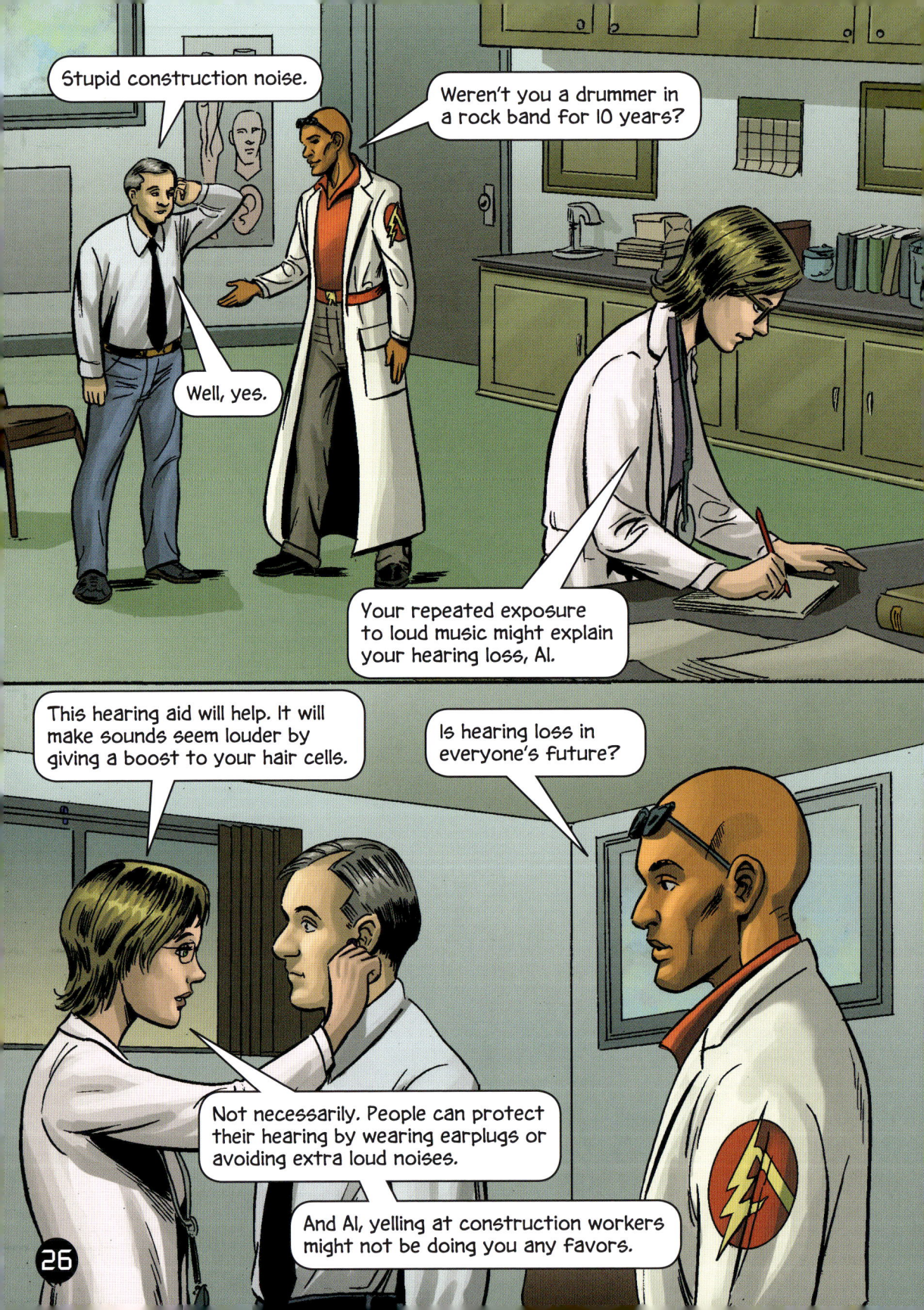

# MORE ABOUT SOUND

- Sound travels faster through solids than through gases and liquids. Why? Because the molecules in solids are packed closer together. The closer the molecules, the faster the sound waves travel from one molecule to the next. A sound travels 770 miles (1,239 kilometers) per hour through air. It speeds through steel at about 11,630 miles (18,716 kilometers) per hour.

- Most bats use echolocation to hunt. As they fly, bats release high pitched sounds that bounce off objects all around them. Based on the echoes they hear, the bats can locate and determine the size of insects fluttering nearby.

- The hammer, anvil, and stirrup are the smallest bones in the human body. They are the same size now as they were the day you were born. All together, they could fit on a penny.

- Ear wax helps keep your ears clean. As wax forms inside the ear canal, it clings to dirt particles. Eventually, the wax works its way out of the ear, carrying the dirt along with it.

- The liquid in the cochlea does more than just magnify vibrations. It also plays a role in balance and helps your body know what is up and what is down.

- Elephants use infrasound, or sound below the range of human hearing, to talk to each other. They can use rumbling sounds as low as 5 Hz to communicate.

- A cricket's hearing organs are located just below the knees of its front legs. A cicada's hearing organ is on its abdomen.

- Scientists measure the loudness, or volume, of sounds in decibels (dB). A whisper measures about 20 dB, while normal talking is 60 dB. A jet measures about 120 dB and a firecracker exploding is about 140 dB. Any sound above 85 dB can cause hearing damage if listened to for too long. At close range, noise levels above 140 dB cause immediate hearing damage.

# SHOEBOX GUITAR

Before you headline a world tour, jam out on this DIY guitar and learn all about the magic world of sound!

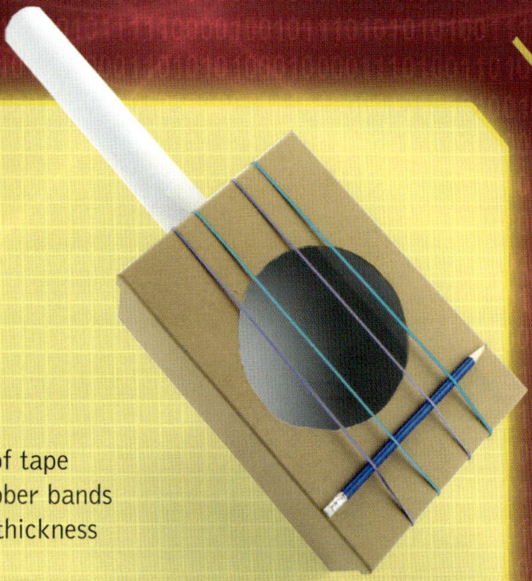

## WHAT YOU NEED:

- pencil
- shoebox
- scissors
- cardboard paper towel tube
- large roll of tape
- 4 large rubber bands of various thickness

## WHAT YOU DO:

1. Use the pencil to punch a hole in the center of one short side on the shoebox. Place one end of the paper towel tube over the hole and trace around it with the pencil.
2. Cut out the circle traced in step 1. Use the hole you punched to start the scissors.
3. Insert the paper towel tube into the hole. Tape the paper towel tube in place to complete the guitar's handle.
4. Use the pencil to punch a hole in the center of the shoebox's top. Draw a large circle around the hole. You may trace the roll of tape as a guide.
5. Cut out the large circle. Use the hole you punched to start the scissors.
6. Wrap the rubber bands around the shoebox lengthwise. Place them in order from widest to thinnest and space them evenly over the large hole.
7. Slide the pencil under the rubber bands just below the hole to create a bridge for the guitar strings.
8. Strum the strings to play the guitar. Try changing the angle of the bridge and the tightness of the rubber bands to make different sounds.

# DISCUSSION QUESTIONS

1. How do the frequencies of high-pitch and low-pitch sounds compare in terms of the number of waves that pass by each second? Discuss the differences and think of two examples of each type of sound.

2. Thunder and lightning always happen together because they are caused by the same electrical event in the atmosphere. Why do you think we always see lightning before we hear the accompanying thunder?

3. What happens when a sound meets a surface or a new material? Discuss three possible things that can happen and explain why they occur.

4. Why is it important for a worker at a construction site to wear ear protection? Discuss your reasons.

# WRITING PROMPTS

1. What is sound? Based on what you've read in this book, write a definition for sound in your own words.

2. Sound travels through air, water, and empty space at different speeds. Write a short paragraph explaining why this is the case.

3. Sound travels from a vibrating object and into your ear. Make a list of the parts of the ear the sound must pass through in order for you to hear it.

4. Bats use sonar to find their food. Draw a diagram of a bat detecting an insect with sound waves that helps explain why this ability is called echolocation.

# TAKE A QUIZ!

# GLOSSARY

absorb (ab-ZORB)—to soak up

cochlea (KOH-klee-uh)—a spiral-shaped part of the ear that helps send sound messages to the brain

decibel (DESS-uh-bel)—a unit for measuring the volume of sounds

eardrum (IHR-druhm)—a thin piece of skin stretched tight like a drum inside the ear; the eardrum vibrates when sound waves strike it.

echolocation (eh-koh-loh-KAY-shuhn)—the process of using sounds and echoes to locate objects; bats use echolocation to find food.

energy (EN-ur-jee)—the ability to do work, such as moving things or giving heat or light

frequency (FREE-kwuhn-see)—the number of sound waves that pass a location in a certain amount of time

hertz (HURTS)—a unit for measuring the frequency of sound wave vibrations; one hertz equals one sound wave per second.

molecule (MOL-uh-kyool)—two or more atoms of the same or different elements that have bonded; a molecule is the smallest part of a compound that can be divided without a chemical change.

pitch (PICH)—the highness or lowness of a sound; low pitches have low frequencies and high pitches have high frequencies.

reflect (ri-FLEKT)—to bounce off an object

refract (ri-FRACT)—to bend when passing through a material at an angle

vibration (vye-BRAY-shuhn)—a fast movement back and forth

# READ MORE

**Johnson, Robin.** *The Science of Sound Waves.* Catch a Wave. New York: Crabtree Publishing Company, 2018.

**Oxlade, Chris.** *Super Science Light and Sound Experiments: 10 Amazing Experiment With Step-by-Step Photographs.* Thaxted, England, Miles Kelly Publishing, 2016.

**Spilsbury, Richard.** *Investigating Sound.* Investigating Science Challenge. New York: Crabtree Publishing Company, 2018.

# INTERNET SITES

Use Facthound to find Internet sites related to this book.

Visit www.facthound.com

Just type in 9781543529449 and go!

Check out projects, games and lots more at www.capstonekids.com

# INDEX

absorbing sound, 19
animals, 10, 11, 16, 22–23
audiologists, 24

ears, 12–13, 19, 23, 24–26, 27
   anvil, 13
   cochlea, 13
   eardrum, 13
   hair cells, 13, 25, 26
   hammer, 13
   stirrup, 13
echoes, 19
echolocation, 22

energy, 7, 9

frequency, 10–11

hearing, 4, 11, 12–13, 16, 17
   and damage, 24–26
hearing aids, 26
hertz, 10, 11

infrasound, 11
intensity, 8

larynx, 8

molecules, 7

outer space, 17

pitch, 10, 11

reflecting sound, 19, 21
refracting sound, 20

safety, 24–26
sonar, 21–22
sonic booms, 15
sound waves, 7, 9, 10, 12, 15, 16, 17, 20, 21, 22
speed, 14–15, 16

ultrasound, 11

vibrations, 7, 8, 10, 13, 17, 28
vocal cords, 8
volume, 8, 9, 10, 25, 26

31901063623054